TWOC

A Play by Mark Morris

Series Editors: Steve Barlow and Steve Skidmore

Heinemann

Heinemann Educational Publishers
Halley Court, Jordan Hill, Oxford OX2 8EJ
Part of Harcourt Education

Heinemann is the registered trademark of
Harcourt Education Limited

First published 2003

07 06 05 04 03
10 9 8 7 6 5 4 3 2 1

British Library Cataloguing in Publication Data is available
from the British Library on request.

ISBN 0 435 21458 6

Illustrations by Andrew Skilleter
Cover photos by Peter Morris
Cover design by Shireen Nathoo Design
Designed and typeset by Artistix, Thame, Oxon
Printed and bound in Great Britain by Biddles Ltd

Tel: 01865 888058 www.heinemann.co.uk

Contents

Note on Sound Effects

There are a lot of sound effects in Scene 2. Some possible ways of creating them include:

1. If you have the equipment, record the effects on a computer or digital recorder, then play back using a keyboard with midi connection.
2. Create the sound effects with musical instruments, for example: urgent drumbeats for the car engine, squealing violin for the brakes, saxophone for police siren.
3. Simplest of all, have the actors create the sound effects themselves. Actors in the car can make engine and brake noises when they are not speaking. Actors offstage can create the more distant effects.

Characters

Alex
Aged 15.
Bright,
intelligent boy
who often
tries to
impress
others

Ben
Alex's friend, aged 14

Kate
Aged 15, Ben's sister and Alex's girlfriend

Keano
Aged 17. Car thief and local thug

Degsy
Aged 17. Keano's friend

Policeman

Scene One

The stage is set as a city street in the early evening. Ben and Alex are standing at opposite sides of the stage, in spotlights or with their backs to each other. They are both talking into mobile phones.

ALEX: Don't worry, I won't be long.

BEN: *(Crossly)* You'd better not be. I've been here ages!

ALEX: *(Becoming annoyed)* Look, Ben, I'm sorry I'm late but there's no need to get funny with me.

BEN: Got a good reason?

ALEX: I couldn't get in the bathroom. You know what my sister's like – she has to spend that long getting ready 'cos she's so ugly.

BEN: Well, I'm not hanging about here getting cold. *(He starts to go off)* I'll go and meet Kate off the bus …

(Ben goes off.)

ALEX: Okay, I'll find you.

(Alex breaks off as Keano and Degsy come on. Keano looks around, on watch. Degsy takes a screwdriver out of his pocket and sneaks off.)

ALEX: Hang on a minute … *(He ducks down and speaks more quietly)* Hey, I'm on Green Lane, and guess what I'm looking at right now? Go on, guess.

BEN: *(Offstage)* How should I know?

ALEX: It's only Keano and Degsy, and they're fiddling with some car across the road from me.

BEN: *(Offstage)* What do you mean 'fiddling'? Breaking in?

ALEX: Looks like it. I bet it's Keano and Degsy nicking all those cars recently. I'm going to watch for a bit – see what happens.

BEN: *(Offstage: worried)* Don't do anything daft.

ALEX: Like what? Nick a Porsche and go for a spin? Don't be stupid. Green Lane. Get yourself down here quick!

(He ends the call. Degsy comes back on and whispers to Keano. They mime trying the door of a car. Alex stands up and walks quietly up behind them.)

ALEX: What you up to then?

(The two boys are startled.)

KEANO: *(Angrily)* Us? What are *you* up to, sneaking up on people like that?

ALEX: Thought I'd see if you two will ever get around to nicking a car. Or are you just inspecting the locks?

DEGSY: *(Laughing)* Cheeky little twerp. Who do you think you are then, matey?

ALEX: I'm Alex. You two used to go to my school. You were older than me though.

KEANO: No kidding? Now clear off before you get a slap.

ALEX: I'm only watching. What you doing, then? Nicking stereos?

DEGSY: Nah, not tonight. Just looking for a laugh.

ALEX: What sort of laugh?

DEGSY: We'll find a car, nick it, then see what happens.

ALEX: I can tell you now what'll happen. You'll get caught and banged up, that's what. Not my idea of a laugh really.

(Keano walks towards Alex and pushes him.)

KEANO: And what do you know about it, Mr Expert?

DEGSY: Lay off him, the kid's got bottle. Look kid, you don't want to hang around here. It's a bit too grown up for you.

ALEX: *(Trying to show off)* Oh yeah? Anyone can nick cars, it's no big deal.

KEANO: *(Laughing)* Really? How many times have you done a TWOC?

ALEX: A what?

DEGSY: T.W.O.C. – Taking Without Owner's Consent.

ALEX: *(Puzzled)* Huh?

KEANO: It just means nicking cars – it's police-talk. Got a bit to learn, haven't you?

ALEX: Maybe. So are you going to show me then?

KEANO: You?

ALEX: Why not?

DEGSY: Yeah, why not? It'll be a laugh. Are you sure you're up for this?

ALEX: *(After a pause)* Sure. Sorted. So what do we do then? What about that one?

DEGSY: Nah, too hard to get into.

ALEX: I thought you were experts.

KEANO: We are, kid, so shut up and listen. That is a new series BMW. 0–60 in 7.2 seconds. Even if you can get into it, jumping the engine means you have to rip out the steering column.

DEGSY: Too much hassle, you see.

ALEX: *(Pointing)* What about that one then?

KEANO: Don't make me laugh! That's a granny wagon. Too slow.

DEGSY: Dead easy to get into, though.

ALEX: What about the alarm?

KEANO: What about it?

ALEX: Won't you set it off?

KEANO: So what if we do? Nobody takes any notice of them. Car alarms go off all the time and nobody even blinks.

DEGSY: And anyway, if we want to get in quietly it's easy enough.

ALEX: Oh yeah? How?

KEANO: Why should we tell you all the tricks of the trade?

DEGSY: *(Threatening)* Or are you trying to say we're thick and don't know how?

ALEX: *(Laughing)* No, no. You're as smart as they come, Degsy.

DEGSY: *(Winking at Keano)* All right, kid. What do you fancy?

KEANO: How about a four by four? Bit of off-road should be a laugh. We could take it through the park and go rallying over the school fields.

DEGSY: Nah, let's go for pure speed. Let's get a Mercedes.

KEANO: Too flash.

DEGSY: Okay – what about a Subaru? There's one parked at the end of the street.

KEANO: Good call. You coming, kid?

ALEX: *(Hesitating)* Err … I'm not sure. I'm supposed to be … er … meeting some mates.

KEANO: Told you he was a wimp. Got no bottle, kid?

ALEX: Plenty, thanks. I'll just wait here for them. You come back and … er … pick me up when you've got the car.

KEANO: *(Sneering)* And you'll still be here, will you?

DEGSY: Course he will. You're up for a giggle, aren't you kid?

ALEX: Yes … er … definitely. Can't wait.

(Keano and Degsy exit, laughing to each other. Alex puts his head in his hands.)

ALEX: *(To himself)* What are you doing, you plonker? Your gob is going to get you in some serious hassle before long.

(Ben and Kate enter. They begin to nudge each other when they see Alex talking to himself.)

ALEX: Why can't you just learn to keep it shut?

BEN: *(Sniggering)* That's a good idea, mate, or else people could think you're a bit of a loony.

KATE: *(Laughing)* But not us, of course. *(She kisses Alex on the cheek)*

ALEX: Okay, okay, very funny. I didn't see you, did I?

KATE: Who were you talking to anyway?

ALEX: Oh … er … no one. Just myself. No one else.

BEN: So where are Keano and Degsy, then? You said they were down here nicking cars.

ALEX: That's the problem.

BEN: What's the problem?

ALEX: Keano and Degsy. They've just gone off to rob a car. Then they're coming back here for me.

BEN: You what? Are you mad? Do you want to end up wrapped around a lamppost? Those two are complete nutters.

KATE: You say and do some mad things, Alex, but this is no joke.

ALEX: Er … course it is. It's easy. We're just going for a little ride.

BEN: *(Suddenly)* Watch it.

(A Policeman comes on and walks towards the teenagers.)

POLICEMAN: Can you tell me what you're doing hanging around here?

BEN: Not much. We've just met up.

KATE: We're all going to the Youth Club disco on King Street. I'm Kate, this is Ben, my brother, and this is Alex, my boyfriend. *(She links arms with Alex)*

POLICEMAN: Have you seen anyone hanging around the cars on this street? We've had a couple of phone calls from the local neighbourhood watch.

BEN: *(Shaking his head)* No. Nothing.

KATE: Definitely not, but we've only been here a minute.

POLICEMAN: What about you, son?

ALEX: *(Quietly)* No.

POLICEMAN: Well if you do, phone the station. We think they're the same joyriders as last week.

KATE: *(Staring hard at Alex)* Sure. Of course we will. I can't stand those macho posers. Brains in their backsides, if you ask me.

(The Policeman smiles and walks on.)

ALEX: The coppers will never catch them, they're much too smart.

BEN: *(Laughing)* Keano and Degsy? Your average garden gnome has got more brains than those two.

ALEX: Who's talking about brains? They're top drivers! Speed freaks! Schumacher couldn't catch them.

KATE: *(Amazed)* What is the matter with you? Are you drunk?

ALEX: Don't be daft.

KATE: *(To Ben)* He's about to get in a stolen car with two brain-dead morons and he calls me daft! Is this some macho thing, Alex? Are you trying to impress me or something?

ALEX: No, I was just saying they were good drivers.

KATE: Good? Because they drive fast?

ALEX: *(Smiling)* Exactly.

KATE: Well, you might think that's good driving. Personally I think getting there alive is more important.

ALEX: *(Trying to make a joke)* Woman driver!

KATE: *(Angrily)* It's men who kill on the roads, you know, not women. So what if we go slower? It's better than being dead. Why are you showing off like this?

ALEX: I'm not. It's just that … er …

(Sound effects: a car travelling fast. It screeches to a halt.)

DEGSY: *(Running on stage)* Look sharp, kid, this isn't a taxi, you know.

ALEX: See you later, Kate. Have fun at your soppy disco.

(Alex and Degsy run off stage. Sound effects: two car doors slam and the car screams away.)

Scene Two

The stolen car. Keano is driving, Degsy sits in the passenger seat. Alex is in the back seat.

(The stolen car is represented by four chairs set out as car seats.)

ALEX: *(Nervously)* So what do we do now, then?

DEGSY: Find some fun, that's what. With this beauty there's nothing on the road to catch us.

KEANO: Watch this, kid!

(Sound effects: squeal of brakes. Alex, Keano and Degsy lean forward.)

DEGSY: Mmm, smell that rubber.

ALEX: *(Amazed)* What're you doing? This car is nicked and you're making everyone look at us.

KEANO: *(Laughing)* He's as sharp as a razor, this one! That's the whole point, you little prat. How are the police going to chase us if they don't know where we are?

ALEX: You're kidding, right?

DEGSY: All we have to do is cause a bit of fuss around here and some old fogey will ring PC Plod. Then the fun starts.

ALEX: Fun?

DEGSY: Yeah. It's alright doing this for a bit. Bit of rallying, a few skids and handbrake turns. But there's nothing like the chase.

KEANO: That really gets the blood pumping.

ALEX: But what if we get caught?

KEANO: No chance of that, not with me behind the wheel.

ALEX: Oh, sure. They have trained, expert drivers, high-performance cars, helicopters and radar. We've got you. Passed your test, have you?

KEANO: Who needs a test? Tests are for girls.

(Sound effects: the car sets off again, wheels spinning.)

ALEX: Slow down you idiot! You'll hit something.

(Sound effects: the brakes screech. There are some loud bumps as the car mounts the kerb. The boys slide around in the car.)

KEANO: That got some curtains flapping. Look at 'em. Time for a little music, I think. *(He mimes turning on the stereo and loud music blasts out)*

DEGSY: Just drive up and down a bit and pull a few handbrakes. They'll ring the coppers then.

(Alex puts his hands over his head and shouts.)

ALEX: No!

(Sound effects: a car going into a screeching, high-speed spin. Alex is thrown from one side of the back seat to the other.)

ALEX: *(Screaming)* SLOW DOWN, WILL YOU! This is mental …

(The three boys lean forward again, as Keano steps on the brake.)

KEANO: *(Shouts)* Shut it, kid. Kill that music.

(Degsy mimes switching the music off.)

KEANO: Listen.

(Sound effects: a police siren heard in the distance.)

ALEX: Great. Just great.

DEGSY: Ladies and gentlemen, I think that's our cue. Shall we dance?

KEANO: Certainly, sir. Warp factor eight coming up.

(Sound effects: loud engine revs. Looking terrified, Alex sits back and mimes clicking on a seat belt.)

DEGSY: There they are, coming out of Park Road. Floor it, Keano. GO! GO! GO!

(Sound effects: car taking off at speed. The boys are flung backwards as Keano accelerates.)

KEANO: *(Shouts)* WHERE? WHERE? I'm going for the by-pass.

(Sound effects: the brakes screech as the car speeds dangerously along the street.)

ALEX: *(Looking behind)* They're right up your backside.

KEANO: *(Laughing)* Well, open the boot for them then!

DEGSY: Put your foot down, Keano, and stop messing about. We can murder that thing they're driving in second gear.

KEANO: Wave 'em goodbye.

(He mimes pulling the 'steering wheel' over hard. The boys are flung violently to the right.)

ALEX: *(Screaming)* What you going into the park for?

DEGSY: Calm down, kid, we've got four-wheel drive. We'll leave 'em for dead in here.

ALEX: Mind the flower beds – at least stick to the grass!

KEANO: Soz, Alan Titchmarsh!

DEGSY: *(Looking back)* Hey! They're stuck! *(Laughing)* They've got stuck on that grass bank.

KEANO: Told you, kid! Told you they can't get me.

ALEX: Okay, okay, you made your point, just take me back. Let me out of the car.

KEANO: Oh, I don't think that's right, do you Degsy? We're not finished yet.

(Sound effects: the car skids noisily.)

DEGSY: *(Shouting)* THAT WAY! Through the flower beds and out the main gates.

ALEX: *(Screaming)* NO, NOT THAT WAY, you'll go straight into the traffic, you'll hit something.

KEANO: Not me, kiddo. Watch this!

(Sound effects: more skidding.)

ALEX: We're on the wrong side of the road! Turn us round! Turn us round!

DEGSY: Move it, move it! That lorry's going to hit us.

KEANO: Keep your teeth in, I'm sorted.

(Sound effects: the car screeches away. A police siren is heard.)

DEGSY: We've got another copper, this one's in a big Volvo.

KEANO: Ooooo! Serious stuff, eh? Throwing the big boys at us, are we?

ALEX: This is mad, you pair are totally mad! Stop this car now, for God's sake!

KEANO: Stop whining, little boy. Do your pampers need changing?

ALEX: Stop the damn car NOW. Let me out, let me out NOW! *(Screaming)* PLEASE! Come on lads, you've had your fun, now let me out before …

DEGSY: Watch out – police!

(Sound effects: the car skids noisily. The boys are jogged around.)

DEGSY: We're on the pavement. Look out for that gang of kids, LOOK OUT!

(Sound effects: teenagers screaming, and a loud thud.)

ALEX: *(Whispering, in shock)* What happened? What did you do?

KEANO: *(Sounding a little shaky)* Missed them, what do you think?

ALEX: I don't think you did. I heard a noise.

KEANO: *(More confidently)* We hit the wall, that was all.

ALEX: You sure? Didn't sound like that to me.

(Sound effects: a helicopter overhead. Degsy leans forward to look up through the windscreen.)

DEGSY: Oh hell, Keano, look up there. They've got the big bird out after us.

KEANO: Where is it? Which way now?

DEGSY: *(Looking back)* More coppers behind. A Volvo and a Beamer.

KEANO: *(Leaning forward to look up through the windscreen)* Where's that damn bird got to? Is it behind or in front? *(He looks over his shoulder)*

DEGSY: Watch the road, man, stop looking for that bird. *(Screaming)* WATCH THE ROAD!

KEANO: *(Looking up, wildly)* Still can't see it, where's it …

ALEX: The lorry …

(Alex and Degsy scream and brace themselves. All the lights go out. Sound effects: a huge crash. When the stage lights come up, Keano is looking dazed, Degsy is clutching his head, and Alex is lying back in his seat.)

DEGSY: *(Coughing and shaking Keano)* Get out, get out.

KEANO: *(Moving slowly, in pain)* Where's the kid, where is he?

DEGSY: *(Looks round)* He's had it. Looks dead to me. Now drag him into the front and leg it.

(With much grunting and groaning, Keano and Degsy haul Alex into the driver's seat. They stumble away. Alex remains unconscious inside the car.)

SCENE THREE

A private room in a hospital. Alex is lying asleep in bed. Kate and Ben sit beside him.

BEN: It might have been better if he'd stayed in the coma.

KATE: *(Quietly)* What do you mean? He was out for over a week. Isn't that enough punishment?

BEN: I don't mean punishment. Come on Kate, think about it. It might have been better for *everyone* if he stayed in that coma.

KATE: No, it's not fair.

BEN: He's my friend too, you know, but think about it. We don't know whether he'll ever be able to use that arm again – and he'll have a death on his conscience too.

KATE: It's just not fair. He was only showing off.

(Alex begins to wake up.)

KATE: *(Trying to speak brightly)* Hi, Alex. How are you feeling?

BEN: Yeah, mate. You OK?

ALEX: *(Very quietly)* Bit better. I can remember a bit more but it's still very fuzzy though.

KATE: That's good. *(She bites her lip and looks at Ben)*

(Alex tries to move but cannot.)

ALEX: What's wrong with my arm? *(Louder)* Why can't I feel anything there?

KATE: It's alright, calm down. It's the coma you were in, that's all.

BEN: *(Trying to distract him)* What can you remember?

ALEX: *(Slowly)* Not much really. Those two nutters wouldn't stop. Then there was a police car. I think we hit something.

KATE: You could say that. You were out cold for ten days.

ALEX: But that doesn't explain why my arm feels like … well … like nothing at all, like it's not there.

KATE: *(Softly)* There's a reason you can't feel very much, Alex.

(There is a long pause.)

ALEX: Go on.

KATE: *(Looking at Ben)* I'm not … er … sure I should be the one to tell you. Perhaps the doctor could …

ALEX: *(Sharply)* Tell me.

KATE: The eight hours you were in surgery … There's a lot of damage to your lower spine … It's still too early to tell …

ALEX: Tell what? I'll be able to walk, won't I?

BEN: The doctors say you might, but it won't be easy.

ALEX: Might?

KATE: You nearly died, Alex. Be grateful you're alive.

ALEX: But what about my arm?

BEN: They had to operate. It was pretty badly smashed up. There was nerve damage, or something like that. They … er …

ALEX: What? Tell me.

KATE: *(After a deep breath)* They say there's nothing they could do for it.

ALEX: What do you mean, there's nothing they could do for my arm? It's still there, isn't it? When will it work again?

BEN: *(Very quietly)* It won't.

(There is the sound of angry voices outside the door. Among the shouts can be heard 'He's a murderer' and 'I'll kill him myself'.)

ALEX: What's all that about?

KATE: Oh … er … nothing. Nothing to do with us.

ALEX: Who's a murderer? Who are they talking about?

BEN: Nothing. Don't worry yourself about it. Try and rest a bit.

(A door opens and a Policeman enters.)

POLICEMAN: *(To Alex)* Oh, you're awake again, are you? Good, my sergeant wants to speak with you.

BEN: What's going on out there?

POLICEMAN: *(Looking at Alex)* Just some people involved in the case.

ALEX: The case? What case?

BEN: Don't talk to him, Alex. Your lawyer said …

ALEX: Lawyer?

POLICEMAN: *(To Ben)* You've got it wrong, son. I'm not the investigating officer. I'm his police protection.

ALEX: Protection?

KATIE: Alex, you shouldn't say anything until your mum and dad get here …

ALEX: Look, I didn't steal the car. I only went with them, with Keano and Degsy, I mean.

POLICEMAN: Are you sure? That's not exactly what they say.

ALEX: We had a crash, didn't we?

POLICEMAN: They said it was you that had the crash. They said you were driving.

ALEX: That's not true.

BEN: *(Stands to face the Policeman)* He's right. He wasn't driving when he left us.

POLICEMAN: I understand what you're trying to do. You're good friends with Alex.

KATE: What do you mean?

POLICEMAN: Maybe he wasn't driving when he left you, but what was to stop him taking over the wheel later?

ALEX: I'm telling you I wasn't driving. I can't drive!

POLICEMAN: You were there. You were found in the driver's seat. That will be more than enough for the court.

ALEX: The driver's seat? I don't understand … Look, I've told you. I didn't really want to go with them. They stole the car. They're the ones who smashed it up.

POLICEMAN: Stealing a car is the least of your problems, young man. I'm afraid it's a little more serious than that.

ALEX: Eh? *(To Kate and Ben)* What's he talking about?

(Kate and Ben do not reply. They both stare at the floor.)

POLICEMAN: I'm talking about the girl your car hit.

ALEX: Girl? What girl? We never hit anyone … unless …

POLICEMAN: Go on.

ALEX: When we … er … skidded into a wall … I think … near a group of kids. We didn't hit them. *(More quietly)* I'm sure we didn't hit them.

POLICEMAN: I'm afraid it didn't happen quite like that.

ALEX: *(Louder)* It must have. We didn't hit anyone.

(Silence. Everyone stares at Alex.)

ALEX: I didn't mean anything, it was just a laugh, just a joyride.

KATE: *(Sharply)* Joyride? Just a laugh? Of all the stupid names for what you did – 'joyriding'! *(Sadly)* There's not much 'joy' in it for those people outside.

ALEX: What people outside? What's he on about?

KATE: That shouting from earlier, it's ... er ...

ALEX: Well? *(He hits the bed in frustration)* What's happening? Tell me.

POLICEMAN: The people outside are the parents and family of Rebecca Bradman.

ALEX: Who's she? Never heard of her.

POLICEMAN: They've heard of you. She was the young girl that you and your friends killed during your 'joyride'. She was fourteen years old.

ALEX: Oh God.

POLICEMAN: She didn't die straight away. She hung on for days before she gave up. She passed away last night, that's why her parents are here.

ALEX: But I didn't mean anything ... it was just a laugh.

POLICEMAN: You keep saying that. But nobody's laughing, are they? Cars aren't a joke, son. In the hands of morons like you they're just half a ton of killing machine.

ALEX: This isn't happening. It's not real.

POLICEMAN: *(Firmly)* I'm afraid it is, and you're going to have to get used to it. The doctors think your own injuries won't get any better.

ALEX: I didn't mean anyone to get hurt.

POLICEMAN: The girl's parents out there would tear you to pieces if they could. That's why I'm here. Mind you, if it was up to me – I'd let them.

(The Policeman leaves the room.)

ALEX: *(To Ben and Kate)* Tell him, tell him I didn't mean it.

KATE: You were the one who said good driving meant fast driving.

BEN: I'm sorry, but what do you want me to say?

KATE: *(Picking up her bag)* We'd better be going. Come on, Ben.

ALEX: Don't go, stay with me. Please. *(He grabs Kate's hand)* Please stay, I need my friends.

BEN: *(Looking at the floor)* Sorry. Come on, Kate.

(Kate pulls away from Alex and leaves the room with Ben. Alex is left on his own.)

ALEX: *(Quietly, to himself)* But I didn't mean it … I didn't mean to hurt anyone … anyone.